Give 'Em What They Want !

Managing the Public's Library

The Baltimore County Public Library's
BLUE RIBBON COMMITTEE

The Public Library Administration Series

American Library Association
Chicago and London
1992

The paper used in this publication meets the minimum requirements of American National Standard for Information Sciences—Permanence of Paper for Printed Library Materials, ANSI Z39.48-1984.∞

Composed by Alexander Typesetting, Inc. in Optima and Palatino on Datalogics Pagination System and Linotron 202.
Printed on 50-pound Finch Opaque, a pH neutral stock, and bound in 10-point C1S cover stock by Edwards Brothers, Inc.

Library of Congress Cataloging-in-Publication Data

Give 'em what they want! : managing the public's library / the Baltimore County Public Library's Blue Ribbon Committee.
p. cm. — (The Public library administration series)
Includes bibliographical references.
ISBN 0-8389-0592-7
1. Public libraries—Administration. 2. Public relations—Libraries. I. Baltimore County Public Library. Blue Ribbon Committee. II. Series.
Z678.G57 1992
025.1'974—dc20 92-13756
CIP

Printed in the United States of America.

96 95 94 93 92 5 4 3 2 1

CONTENTS

ACKNOWLEDGMENTS

Many people helped us write this book. Our co-workers in BCPL, in the branches and in the administrative offices, both helped us in many ways and tolerated our frantic rush to meet deadlines—we never realized writing a book would take so much time, attention, and concentration!

While almost all of us wrote on our own MACs, the text was coordinated by Catherine Hallameyer and the file server was set up by Jim DeArmey to ease our efforts. Pat Erdman and Ruth Schaefer designed the cover and took the photographs.

Ron Dubberly, Director of the Atlanta-Fulton Public Library, and Bonnie Smothers, Editor, ALA Books, not only persuaded us, against our better judgment, to write this book, but tried to make it readable by detailed and helpful editing. Nevertheless, any errors or omissions are ours, not theirs.

Both Ron and Bonnie were unenthusiastic about our author: The BCPL's Blue Ribbon Committee. Catalogers will probably agree. But we insisted, because our feeling of joint responsibility is strong (no chapter was solely the product of one person), catalogs don't list multiple authors anyway, and all of us subscribe to the BCPL way: share the blame and the credit!

The BCPL's Blue Ribbon Committee

DEDICATION

This book, the philosophy of public library service it attempts to describe, the practice of this philosophy at the Baltimore County Public Library, and the work of the staff which carries out the practice, including all of us, would have been impossible without the enthusiastic support and encouragement of

THE BOARD OF LIBRARY TRUSTEES FOR BALTIMORE COUNTY

Since the library's establishment in 1948, the following 34 members of our governing Board have given their time, their knowledge, their advice, and their leadership toward the goal of an effective and efficient public library service to their fellow citizens.

They are appreciated.

The BCPL's Blue Ribbon Committee

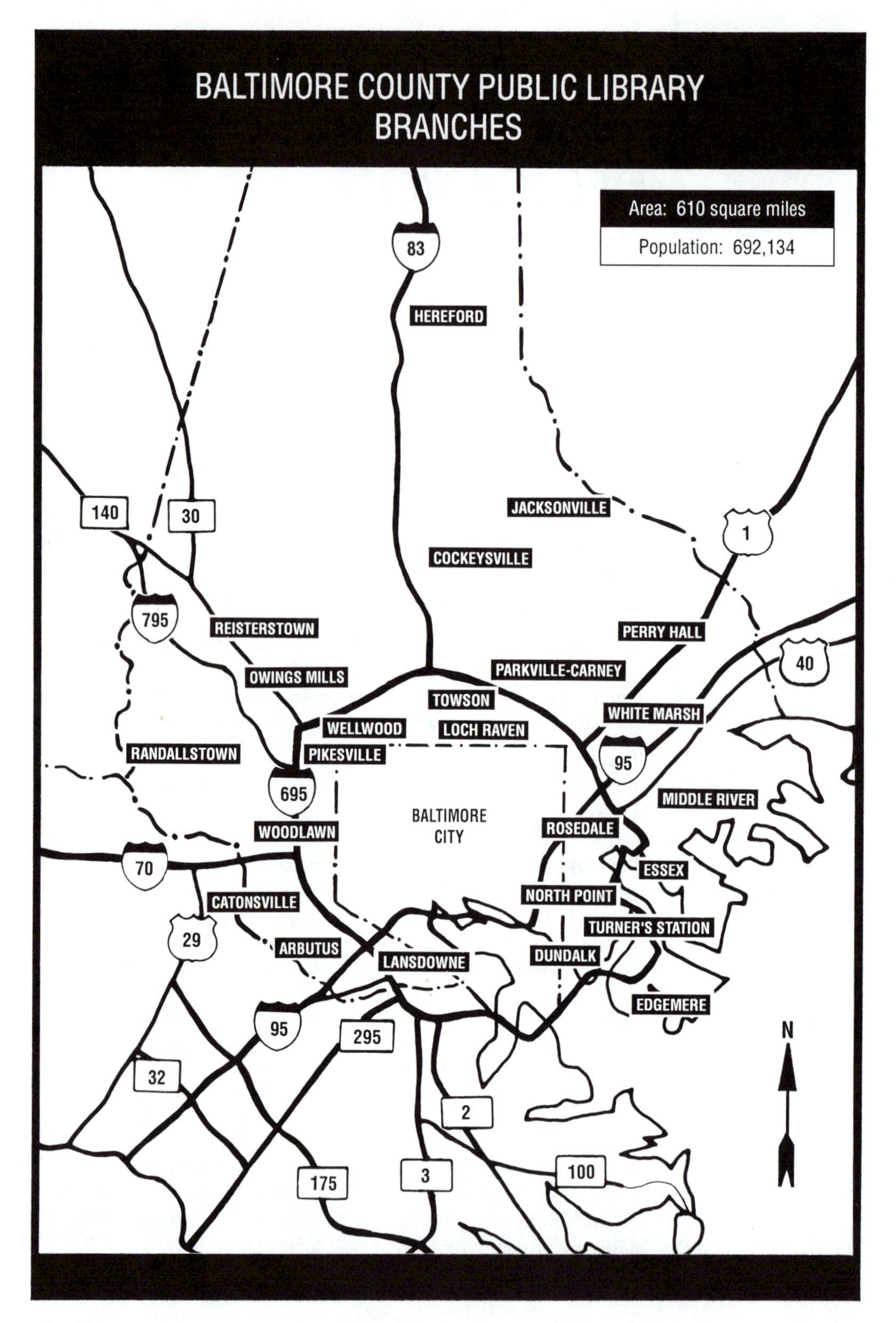

BALTIMORE COUNTY PUBLIC LIBRARY
BRANCHES
Area: 610 square miles
Population: 692,134
83
HEREFORD
JACKSONVILLE
COCKEYSVILLE
140
30
1
795
REISTERSTOWN
PERRY HALL
OWINGS MILLS
PARKVILLE-CARNEY
40
TOWSON
WHITE MARSH
WELLWOOD
LOCH RAVEN
RANDALLSTOWN
PIKESVILLE
95
695
MIDDLE RIVER
BALTIMORE
CITY
WOODLAWN
ROSEDALE
70
ESSEX
CATONSVILLE
NORTH POINT
TURNER'S STATION
29
ARBUTUS
LANSDOWNE
DUNDALK
EDGEMERE
95
295
N
32
2
175
3
100

BALTIMORE COUNTY, MARYLAND

If you're looking at a map of Baltimore City and County, you can imagine that the small rectangle of the city (80 square miles) is a face, and the county (610 square miles) is a helmet around the head, coming down over both ears, with the mark of a chin strap denoting a tunnel across the Baltimore harbor. Some folks say that the resemblance is that of a crab claw wrapped around the city. Either picture sets up in your mind the close proximity of the county to all but a small part of the city's boundaries. Each is a separate political jurisdiction. The county has no incorporated towns or cities, so to all intents and purposes it functions as a city. An elected County Executive is equivalent to a Mayor, and there is an elected County Council. An appointed County Administrative Officer responsible to the County Executive handles the day-to-day administration of the county.

The county is predominantly urban in character with about one-fifth of the land in agricultural cultivation, primarily in the northern end. An interstate beltway encircles the county close to the city's borders and slips by tunnel through the Baltimore city harbor. Major roads run from the city into the county with two interstate highways traversing the full length of the county. A subway and light rail system also serve some of the areas paralleling the two interstate highways.

Population growth, which was booming in the immediate post World War II decades, began to slack off in the 1970s and from 1980 to 1990 grew by 5.6 percent. The U.S. Census figure for the 1990 population is 692,134. Trends can be noted in this population that differ from the times of its greatest growth. Now, the school age population (persons five to 17 years of age) has declined to 103,882, although elementary school age children of the "baby boomlet" in the 1980s are now entering school. Twenty-one percent of the population is under 18 years of age. The major age group is from 18 to 44 years of age and constitutes 43.6 percent of the population. Persons 65 and over are 14 percent of the population. The average household size in 1990 was 2.53. Female-headed family households represent 11.1 percent of all households, and nonfamily households account for 29.2 percent of all households. Whites account for 84.9 percent of the County's population and blacks are 12.3 percent. No other ethnic group exceeds 2.2 percent.

The Baltimore County Public Library was established in 1948 through an amalgamation of small, independent, community-based libraries. Governance is by an administrative Board of Library Trustees whose seven members are appointed by the County Executive (from a list submitted by the Board) for five-year terms subject to one renewal. In the County Charter, the library is listed as one of the county departments, but the provisions of law under which the board operates are found in the Laws of Maryland. The Division of Library Development and Services, a part of the Maryland State Department of Education, has specific responsibilities for the leadership and guidance of school and public libraries in Maryland.

The Baltimore County Public Library is an all-branch library system. This results primarily from a political decision. In a county with no incorporated towns, each community holds itself as equal to any other in terms of services sought from the county. Why alienate people by designating any library facility as a central library? As a practical matter, the building program for branch libraries put the facilities where the people were then located in the early 1960s. With one exception the plan was followed in good detail. The library for Towson, the county seat and approximate geographic center of the county, was left for final much-needed relocation and upgrade. This was done as much to quiet any concerns that this was a favored site for a "Central Library" as because of the difficulties in securing the site.

The staff in 1992 consisted of 361 full-time and 150.5 part-time FTEs. 380.5 FTEs are in branch service (65.50 master degree librarian, 84 paraprofessional librarian, and 231 clerical); 106 FTEs are in technical services and administrative office departments, and 25 FTEs in maintenance and delivery service. Custodial services are given on a contractual basis. No unions exist in BCPL. There is an active staff association with 503 members.

In June 1991 569,944 persons were registered for library service in BCPL—433,689 adults and 136,255 children. About 78,000 of these registrants were residents of Baltimore City who accounted for 12.5 percent of the Library's total circulation in FY91 of 12,863,378. There is reciprocity of the use of library cards throughout all public libraries in Maryland. The 23 counties and independent Baltimore City each have one public library system, so the planning and implementation of public library services can be done with 24 directors and the head of the Division of

Library Development and Services, an asset not found in many other states.

The materials collection consisted in June 1991 of 1,300,000 cataloged and classified volumes; 306,500 paperbacks; 106,300 audiocassettes; 24,300 compact discs; and 60,500 videocassettes. The loan period is 21 days with one renewal period, except for videos.

PREFACE

Public library administrators and managers generally don't write books. It's even hard to get them to write articles for professional periodicals, if the editors of these periodicals are to be believed. Why? Because, unlike their colleagues in the academic area, there is no motivation in the form of either recognition or reward, whether the reward is promotion or money, or both. Books published by the American Library Association or other library-focused presses, and sold through their standing order plans, are found on library shelves throughout the country, generally in the "professional collection." In my experience, however, I have found very, very few public librarians who have read any of these books and they have had little impact on the day-to-day practice of provision of service in the public library.

Speaking at professional conferences is something else: ALA and its public library division, the Public Library Association, together with the state library associations and hundreds of workshops and other in-service efforts, have a never-ending appetite for speakers on public library topics. It matters little whether the speaker knows much about the topic, has anything new to contribute, or can present information so that it can be understood by an audience; you have to have speakers to present a program at a conference, and volunteers are always welcome.

It's a tribute to our profession that about 70 percent of speakers on public library subjects are pretty good and the audience goes away either informed, entertained, or enraged, the result of which is the improvement of, or at least changed, service to the public.

Then why this book, which, if this editor is correct, will be read by few and have little impact on library service? Because all of the members of the BCPL's Blue Ribbon Committee have a more than usual allocation of three concepts: loyalty, duty, and hope.

Loyalty to the stated mission of PLAs Public Library Development Project, that of the "improvement of the effectiveness of public library management," and also to Ronald Dubberly (currently the Director of the Atlanta-Fulton Public Library), a colleague, former coworker, and guru of public library service philosophy, who prevailed upon the Committee to produce this book.

Duty to their profession, their own institution, their own vision of library service, their professional association, and to the Baltimore County Public Library Foundation, which will receive the royalties, if any, from this book.

Hope that other members of the profession who read this book will find ideas, techniques, and inspiration which will improve their own performance and the effectiveness of their library's service to the public. And, not incidentally, that the book will reduce the number of questionnaires and letters which ask "how?" or "why?" do you people do this, or that, and what are the results? We can just refer them to this book—at least until it gets out of date.

All the members of the BCPL's Blue Ribbon Committee are recognized, experienced professionals in their field—and many of them in other fields within the profession as well. All of them have spoken frequently at professional conferences and workshops, informing, entertaining, or enraging their audiences, depending upon their personal styles. I have great personal and professional respect for them (or they wouldn't appear in this book), but so do their coworkers and their colleagues throughout the profession. They have something to say, something to contribute, a track record of the management of library service in the public's library which brings into reality the very best concepts of *Give 'Em What They Want*, and the very best techniques for implementation of those concepts.

At least for now: all of these contributors are known for their complete lack of resistance to change, so don't hold them, or me, to any basic commitment to anything other than public service. The public's concept of service changes, whether because of demographics, technology, financial resources, or a myriad of other factors.

Read this book quickly, before the world of public libraries changes, and with it the techniques of public library management.

Charles W. Robinson
Member, BCPL's Blue Ribbon Committee
and
Director, Baltimore County Public Library

FOREWORD

It is not enough for public library managers to do the right things. They also must do things right. Successful public library service depends more on *effective* managers and administrators than it does on any other resource. Without effective management, other resources will be wasted.

About the Series

This series' aim is to improve public library service by increasing management competence. The strategy is to share effective ways of thinking, key processes for obtaining needed information and taking appropriate action, and current superior methods and techniques.

Practical by design, this series of titles emphasizes achieving preferred results, using resources effectively, sustaining accountability, and asserting influence through competency. The series is intended to help managers when they plan services and projects, identify resource needs, allocate available resources, develop a service organization, evaluate effectiveness, and manage administrative responsibilities.

Each title illustrates principles of effective public library administration and describes the best in professional practice. This twin emphasis provides a context to guide actions as well as to give useful methods and action steps. Both are essential. A group of practices without a context is just a laundry list of possibly useful strategies. Context devoid of accompanying practice is just vacuum-packed theory.

Each title's "framework for thinking" will help readers handle the reality of the way things are and assist with getting things the way they should be. This framework includes paradigms, principles, and priorities. The "best professional practices" content will discuss important issues and, for each, highlight critical decision areas and outline practical action steps appropriate for most circumstances.

The main subject of each book will treat one of the following: a major aspect of public library administration; a type of library service; a functional or support area within the library organization; a service role; or an especially effective library.

Give 'Em What They Want!

Give 'Em What They Want . . . will give you what you want to know if you are interested in winners; that is, knowing how the Baltimore County Public Library has accomplished so much—and WHY! The Baltimore County Public Library (BCPL) System was selected for this series not because its primary service role is necessarily right for every community; BCPL was selected because the way it goes about achieving its goals can be instructive to every library.

Give 'Em What They Want (GEWTW) explains what BCPL believes is important to think about and the ways those things need to be considered. Even if the popular library service role is not your highest priority, *GEWTW* contains more than a few nuggets worth pursuing. *GEWTW* shares a very successful management team's way of thinking about resources: their purposes, allocation, and uses.

Among the good BCPL management methods discussed are location criteria for facilities; facility designs for easy use; methods for evaluating collection use; materials selection for usability; a delivery system for a distributed collection; efficient technology use; developing a common vision in a staff; infusing staff development into everyday activities; instilling commitment and producing staff expertise; making timeliness a critical success factor for service delivery; and, including efficiency as a goal for all BCPL endeavors.

GEWTW not only tells what BCPL has done in becoming so successful in its chosen role, but also why. *GEWTW* relates what BCPL believes is important to concentrate on and why it is important. The methods used by BCPL are shared; but more importantly, the ideas behind the methods and the foundation of reasoning for the idea are conveyed. The BCPL framework *for* thinking about managing library services is a very important nugget revealed through the sharing of the exceptional BCPL framework *of* thinking. That outstanding framework is expressed throughout *GEWTW* in ways that are both concrete and conceptual, by example and rationale. *GEWTW* is narrative history and assertive philosophy, technical and human, idealistic and pragmatic—all inextricably intertwined; and, as such, *GEWTW* is pure BCPL.

It is the idealistic, the human, and the philosophical that will be surprising to some who do not really know BCPL or its leaders. Those readers who expect only technique will receive a bonus of firm practical public library philosophy. Those who might expect only a reproach for not having followed the (often inaccurate) stereotype of "the BCPL way" will instead receive the gift of a valuable lesson. One lesson, for some, might be that just as one cannot judge a book by its cover, one should not always judge leaders by their rhetoric alone. Ironically, both the views of BCPL Director Charles W. Robinson and the BCPL demand-oriented reputation have been exaggerated and oversimplified (often by Robinson himself) to the extent that neither are known for what they truly are. *GEWTW* helps explain both enigmas. The often unknown but crucial BCPL team-work approach to its business and the surprising breadth and strength of BCPL's services *and collections* are revealed.

Disclosed is a little known yet basic strategy at BCPL: cost efficiency is built into every function, even at the expense of traditional public library sacred cows. Also revealed is the underlying philosophy of public librarianship that Robinson and the BCPL team have dared to embrace and have made successful: the worthiness of the common person's taste as a legitimate interest for public library response. This has been a heresy for which many librarians cannot forgive Robinson and the BCPL team. It also will be one of his lasting positive legacies.

The unique development of BCPL chronicled in *GEWTW* includes very little about the top administrative duo which has nurtured and developed that incomparable public library systems throughout most of its existence. It is not surprising. Neither Deputy Director Jean Barry Molz nor Director Charles Weld Robinson would have permitted it. However, there can be no denial that their unique and so very successful amalgam of character, expertise, commitment, perseverance, vision, levelheadedness, and boldness created a team without parallel in public library history. Dedicated to the growth of their staff members and committed to cost effective service responding to user demand, Charlie and Jean Barry have transformed lives and library history. They are the prize of the BCPL's Blue Ribbon Team.

Ronald Dubberly, Series Editor
The Public Library Administration Series

1 THE PUBLIC'S LIBRARY

Not many people, either within or without the profession of librarianship, seem to have noticed it yet, but the public's use of the public's libraries has changed drastically in the forty-plus years since World War II. Public libraries themselves have had little to do with this change in the public's use of libraries; many have not yet responded to the change. Worse yet, some continue to tailor their service to the world of 1938, when America was a very different place, demographically, technologically, and socially. The massive social changes that have come about in these areas have had their effect on public libraries and the services they provide. Despite these changes, the mental image of the library, its mission, its building, and its users is much the same in 1992 as it was in 1938 in the minds of not only the public itself, but trustees, administrators, government officials, and many librarians themselves. Many people, perhaps most people, don't use public libraries the way they *say* they use libraries, the way they think about libraries (which they don't do very often), and the way they vote about the financing and support for libraries.

1938 in 1992

In America today, the middle class, whether you describe it financially, socially, or educationally, is in the majority. This is both an economic and political fact. Almost every family with an income of between $25,000 and $100,000 annually, or even more, would describe itself as "middle class," so of course the self-defined middle class is in the majority.

The public library's public now is almost exclusively this middle class. Not the poor. Not the rich. The big middle, where most of the taxes, the public policy, and the votes come from. This fact, of course, brings with it all sorts of social, moral, and political issues that are endlessly discussed in the public press, in our professional periodicals, and in our personal approvals and disapprovals. These issues do not change the fact that the public

A Baltimore County library in 1938

library's public is almost exclusively middle class, and has been since at least 1938. Never mind that at one time public libraries may have been seen as the immigrants' way to education and to assimilation in society. Probably Carnegie changed all that when he financed the building of hundreds of library buildings right in the neighborhoods of the emerging middle-class populations of cities, the commercial and industrial creators of the middle class. He meant to assist the upwardly mobile immigrant, like himself. His libraries served the emerging middle class.

Demographics have changed. Whether we approve or disapprove, whether we see the transformation of the metropolitan areas as disastrous or whether we just don't care, the America of 1938 is no more and the public library of 1938 is no more, either. Or if it is, it shouldn't be, and its life is continued because public libraries don't cost very much in the total tax picture. And they don't go totally broke, whether the service they give is relevant to demand or not.

There are many, many reasons, or theories, or opinions, given by experts, politicians, and almost anyone else, for the economic decline of central cities all across America, whether it be the policies of the Federal Housing Administration in the 50s or 60s, the desire for separate houses on quarter-acre or larger lots, or the changing needs of industry. For the purposes of our